W9-ALM-067

Inventions We Use for

Jane Bidder

GARETH**STEVENS**
GS
PUBLISHING
A Member of the WRC Media Family of Companies

J 790.133
BID

The author would like to thank Marry Bellis of inventors.about.com. for her help in researching this book. Special thanks to Mattel, Inc. for supplying Polly Pocket and Matchbox and Hot Wheels cars.

Please visit our web site at: www.garethstevens.com
For a free color catalog describing Gareth Stevens Publishing's list of
high-quality books and multimedia programs, call 1-800-542-2595 (USA) or
1-800-387-3178 (Canada). Gareth Stevens Publishing's fax: (414) 332-3567.

Library of Congress Cataloging-in-Publication Data

Bidder, Jane.
    Inventions we use for play / by Jane Bidder.
        p. cm. — (Everyday inventions)
    Includes bibliographical references and index.
    ISBN-10: 0-8368-6900-1 — ISBN-13: 978-0-8368-6900-2 (lib. bdg.)
    1. Toys—Juvenile literature. 2. Play—Juvenile literature. I. Title.
    GV1218.5.B53   2006
    790.1'33—dc22   2006004291

This North American edition first published in 2007 by
Gareth Stevens Publishing
A Member of the WRC Media Family of Companies
330 West Olive Street, Suite 100
Milwaukee, WI 53212 USA

This U.S. edition copyright © 2007 by Gareth Stevens, Inc. Original edition copyright © 2006 by Franklin Watts. First published in Great Britain in 2006 by Franklin Watts, 338 Euston Road, London NW1 3BH, United Kingdom.

Watts series editor: Jennifer Schofield
Watts designer: Ross George
Watts picture researcher: Diana Morris
Watts artwork: Ray Bryant
Gareth Stevens editors: Tea Benduhn and Barbara Kiely Miller
Gareth Stevens art direction: Tammy West
Gareth Stevens graphic designer: Dave Kowalski

Picture credits (t=top, b=bottom, l=left, r=right, c=center): Antikensammlung, Staatliche Museen, Berlin/Bildarchiv Preussischer Kulturbesitz: 12b. The British Library, London: 5b, 10b. British Pathé/ITN Stills: 19t. Malcolm Case-Green/Alamy: 24t. Sally Chappel/V & A Museum, London/Art Archive: 16b. Christies Images: front cover. The Computer History Museum, CA, USA: 24b. Duncan Toys: 13b. Sarah Fabian-Baddiel/HIP/Topfoto: 21. Keystone/Topfoto: 25. Mary Evans Picture Library: 22b, 26t. Ray Moller: 4t, 17b, 20t. The National Yo-Yo Museum & Contest, CA, USA: 12t. Nicholas Sapieha, Poggio Petroio Dog Collection/ Art Archive: 10t. Sothebys/AKG Images: 7. Tamiya/The Hobby Company 2005, www.tamiya.com: 19b. Michael Teller/AKG Images: 20b. Yves Tzaud/Photographers Direct: 23. John Warren/Topfoto: 8b. Karl Weatherly/Corbis: 22t. Jerome Yeats/Alamy: 18.

All rights reserved. No part of this book may be reproduced, stored in a retrieval system, or transmitted in any form or by any means, electronic, mechanical, photocopying, recording, or otherwise, without the prior written permission of the copyright holder.

Printed in The United States of America

1 2 3 4 5 6 7 8 9 10 09 08 07 06

Contents

Words that appear in the glossary are
printed in **boldface** type the first
time they occur in the text.

About Inventions

An invention is a **device** or a tool designed and made for the first time. The person who designs the device is called an inventor. This book looks at some of the playful inventions that keep people entertained. It also introduces inventors and shows how inventions people play with have changed over time.

Making Life Fun

Many toys and games were invented to help people relax. People have played the game of chess, for example, since A.D. 700. Although chess is a game that requires **concentration** to play, it can also be an enjoyable way to spend time with a friend.

From One Comes Another

Many inventions change or **develop** from earlier ideas or are improved over time. In A.D. 100, for example, yo-yos were made of terra-cotta, which is heavy **clay**. Much later, in about 1400, yo-yos were made of wood. Today, most yo-yos are made of **plastic**. Some even have lights that glow as the yo-yo moves up and down.

Learning through Play

Many toys were invented to teach children about the adult world or to help with their education. Map puzzles teach children **geography**, and many board games really make the players think! Some toys help people to make up stories. Until the last two hundred years, most toys were made from materials easily found around the house.

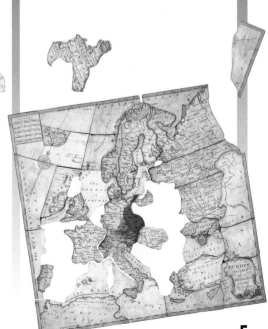

TIME LINE

You will find time lines throughout this book. Use these time lines to keep track of when things happened.

The time lines show, in date order, when specific breakthroughs occurred or particular inventions were introduced. Sometimes, the dates are very exact, but other times, they point to a particular historical era or decade, such as "the 1990s."

Teddy Bears

Teddy bears have not changed much since they were first made more than one hundred years ago. Today, these cuddly toys are still popular with both adults and children.

Going Hunting

In 1902, U.S. president Theodore (Teddy) Roosevelt went hunting. When he refused to shoot a bear cub, the story appeared in a newspaper, showing a cartoon of the president sparing the cub's life. A shopkeeper named Morris Mitchom saw the cartoon, and his wife made a soft toy bear with black buttons for eyes to put in their shop window. Morris put a sign next to the toy that said, "Teddy's Bear." By 1907, most soft toy bears made in the United States and Europe were called teddy bears.

Steiff Bears

Also in 1902, Steiff, a German toy company, made the first soft toy bear that had **jointed** arms and legs. It was shown at the Leipzig Toy Fair in 1903. The bear was seen by an American shop owner who ordered three thousand Steiff bears to sell back home.

Winnie-the-Pooh

In 1921, Christopher Robin Milne received a teddy bear for his first birthday. His father, British author A. A. Milne, saw how his son loved playing with his bear and decided to write a story about a boy, his teddy bear, and other toys. In 1925, Milne published *Winnie-the-Pooh*. Today, Winnie-the-Pooh remains one of the world's best-known teddy bears.

TIME LINE

1902
Morris Mitchom puts a "Teddy's Bear" in his shop window.

1902
The Steiff toy company makes soft toy bears with jointed arms and legs to sell at the Leipzig Toy Fair.

1920
Teddy bears wearing clothes are introduced.

1925
Winnie-the-Pooh is published. It is followed, in 1928, by *The House at Pooh Corner*.

1997
The first Build-a-Bear Workshop® opens in St. Louis, Missouri. At these stores, children can make and dress their own bears or other soft toy animals.

Board Games

There are many exciting board games available today. Some of the most popular games, such as chess and checkers, have been around for hundreds, or even thousands, of years.

Chutes and Ladders

Chutes and Ladders developed from an ancient Indian game called Moksha-Patamu. Some people think the game might have been invented to teach children about good and bad.

Moksha-Patamu became popular in England, in 1892, as Snakes and Ladders (*right*). European settlers introduced it to the United States, where the game later became known as Chutes and Ladders.

Checkers

The game of checkers probably developed from the Egyptian game Alquerque. It was originally played on stone slabs until, in about A.D. 1100, someone used a wooden chess board. In 1535, the French further developed the game and named it Jeu Force. In England, the game of checkers is called draughts.

Chess

People played chess in India and in Persia (now Iran) as early as the eighth century. By the eleventh century, people in Britain were playing chess, and records show that England's King Canute (1016–1035) played it, too. According to a legend, after arguing during a chess game, King Canute had his **opponent** killed.

3500 B.C.
Ancient Egyptians play Senet, which is possibly the oldest board game.

2600–2400 B.C.
Another kind of Senet, the Royal Game of Ur, is played in Mesopotamia (now Iraq).

600 B.C.
Egyptians play Alquerque.

A.D. 700
Chess is played in India and quickly spreads to Persia (now Iran).

1100s
People use wooden chess boards to play checkers.

1980s
Computer chess games are available.

Jigsaw Puzzles

Today, you can find jigsaw puzzles for all ages and interests. But have you ever wondered who first had the idea to cut up a picture and put the pieces together again?

Map Puzzles

In 1767, a London mapmaker named John Spilsbury attached one of his maps to a large piece of wood and cut around the outside of each country with a saw. He cut up the map so children could learn about the countries of the world by putting the pieces of the map together.

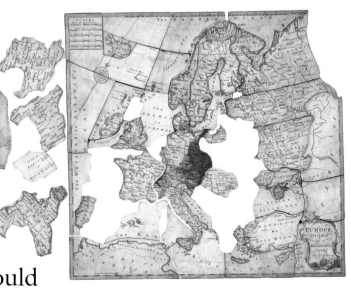

More Pictures

At first, jigsaw puzzles were learning tools, but by 1880, people glued pictures other than maps onto wood and cut them into pieces with saws. By about 1890, people made puzzles out of cardboard as well as wood. By the 1920s and 1930s, companies such as Chad Valley in Britain and Einson-Freeman in the United States were making many different kinds of jigsaw puzzles.

Keeping Busy

In 1932, during the **Great Depression**, weekly jigsaw puzzles were sold on newsstands in the United States. At **25 cents each,** these puzzles were an **inexpensive** way to pass time. At first, only twelve thousand weekly puzzles were made, but at one point, up to two hundred thousand weekly jigsaw puzzles were sold.

TIME LINE

1767
John Spilsbury makes map puzzles.

1890
Jigsaw puzzles are made out of cardboard, as well as wood.

1920s–1930
Companies begin **mass-producing** jigsaw puzzles.

1932
Weekly jigsaw puzzles are sold on newsstands.

1933
Sales of jigsaw puzzles peak at ten million per week in the United States.

Late 1950s
Three-dimensional puzzles are introduced. Instead of laying flat, the puzzles stand upright.

Yo-Yos

It takes practice to master the yo-yo, but once you get the hang of it, this toy is a lot of fun. Some people enter **competitions** to show off their yo-yo skills.

> ### Yo-Yo Fun
> French Emperor Napoleon Bonaparte is said to have enjoyed playing with yo-yos in the late 1700s to relax.

Ancient Yo-Yos

Historians think that the yo-yo may be one of the oldest toys in the world. In fact, yo-yos, appear in pictures found on ancient Greek pottery. Ancient yo-yos were probably made of clay.

Wooden Yo-Yos

The first wooden yo-yos were made in the Philippines in the 1400s. Soon, wooden yo-yos became popular in Africa and Europe. Parents made yo-yos out of common materials for their children to play with.

Donald Duncan's Yo-Yo Company

In 1930, Donald Duncan bought the Yo-Yo Manufacturing Company in California, which was started by Pedro Flores, who was from the Philippines. In the 1950s, Duncan started making yo-yos out of plastic, which was lighter and easier to use than wood. Duncan sent his staff, including Flores, around the United States to show people how to do yo-yo tricks.

TIME LINE

A.D. 100
Early yo-yos are used in ancient Greece.

1400s
Yo-yos are made of wood.

1800s
Children in Britain start playing with yo-yos.

1928
Pedro Flores opens his first yo-yo factory in Santa Barbara, California.

1950s
Donald Duncan's toy company makes plastic yo-yos.

1990s
A yo-yo **craze** sweeps England.

13

Miniature Cars

Miniature **die-cast** cars look just like real cars, only smaller. They have been popular for many years and some people collect them.

Dinky Cars

In the early 1900s, the Dowst Brothers Company in Chicago, Illinois, made the first die-cast miniature car, a Model T Ford. In 1931, Frank Hornby of Meccano, Ltd., began making die-cast miniature cars in Britain. Called Dinky toys, Hornby's miniature cars became one of the best-known brands at the time. People still collect them.

"Dink" to Dinky
The name "Dinky" probably came from the Scottish word *dink*, meaning "cute" or "neat."

Very Small Cars

In the 1950s, the Lesney company in Britain started making die-cast cars that were small enough to fit inside a matchbox. Still popular today, Matchbox cars (*below*) are famous for their high-quality details.

Very Hot Wheels

In 1968, a new kind of miniature car came along. The California toy company Mattel made colorful die-cast hot rods called Hot Wheels. These cars have **low-friction wheels**, which means they can move faster and farther than other toy cars.

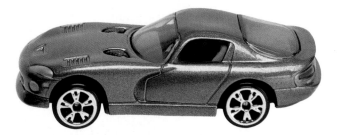

TIME LINE

Early 1900s
The Dowst Brothers Company makes a die-cast miniature Model T Ford.

1931
Frank Hornby designs Dinky toys.

1950s
Lesney introduces Matchbox cars.

1957
Fred Francis invents Scalextric, an electric racing car toy that drives on a track.

1968
Mattel introduces Hot Wheels.

2000s
Miniature cars are still popular, and they are worth money to collectors.

Dolls

Dolls come in all shapes and sizes. Some look just like real babies. Others look like fashion models. Children have played with dolls for at least four thousand years. Over time, dolls have been made from rags, wood, wax, china, rubber, and plastic.

Queen Anne Dolls

By the 1700s, people were making a special kind of dolls with beautiful clothes and jointed legs, but these dolls were made for adult collectors, not children. Known as "Queen Anne" dolls, they were named after the queen of England who ruled from 1702 to 1714.

China Dolls

In the 1840s, many doll makers started making the heads, legs, and arms for their dolls out of china. The heads were often sold separately so children could choose the heads they wanted for their new dolls. Because china breaks easily, children had to be very careful when they played with these dolls.

Polly Pocket

In 1983, an Englishman named Chris Wiggs designed a doll that was small enough to fit in his daughter's pocket. Six years later, this doll, Polly Pocket, appeared in stores. These tiny plastic dolls with removable clothes are now made by the toy company Mattel.

TIME LINE

2000 B.C.
Egyptian children play with cloth dolls.

A.D. 1200
Some dolls are now made of wood.

1700s
Wooden dolls are made with moveable legs. Dolls are also made of wax.

1840s
Dolls are made with soft fabric bodies and china arms, legs, and heads.

1900s
Dolls are made of all kinds of materials.

1959
Barbie is introduced and becomes the best-selling brand-name toy of all time.

1989
The first Polly Pocket doll goes on sale.

Radio-Controlled Toys

A radio-controlled toy is a small version, or **scale model**, of an airplane, car, or boat that is controlled by a **radio transmitter**. A person holds the transmitter a few feet (meters) away so the toy appears to be moving on its own.

Super Quick!
Nitromethane, or "nitro," is a fuel used for some scale models. It is the same fuel used in some real race cars.

Radio-Controlled Boats

In 1898, a scientist named Nikola Tesla held a public demonstration, in New York City, of the first radio-controlled boat. Radio technology controlled the steering and **propulsion** of the boat. Radio-controlled boats are still popular toys for children and adults today.

First Flight

The first officially recorded model airplane flight was made by British Colonel H. J. Taplin in 1957. Colonel Taplin designed and built the plane himself.

Spin Dizzies

Radio-controlled cars were first made in the 1940s. Because these cars could move only in circles, they were called "spin dizzies." In 1974, the Japanese toy company Tamiya started selling models that moved in straight lines. The new models launched a fun new pastime.

TIME LINE

1898
Nikola Tesla demonstrates a radio-controlled boat.

1940s
The first radio-controlled cars appear.

1957
Colonel H. J. Taplin flies the first radio-controlled airplane in England.

1974
Tamiya launches a radio-controlled M4 Sherman Tank, which sparks enthusiasm for radio-controlled toys.

1976
Tamiya introduces a radio-controlled Porsche 934.

2005
The Tomy toy company models a radio-controlled Beetle after Herbie the Beetle in the Disney film *Herbie: Fully Loaded.*

Train Sets

Soon after steam trains were invented in the 1840s, people began making toy trains for children. The first toy trains were made of wood, and children pushed them across the floor. Today, most train sets are made of plastic or metal, and they are powered by electricity.

Magical Marklin

In 1891, German toy company Marklin started selling toy trains and the tracks to go with them. At first the Marklin trains were wind-up toys. Later, they were powered by steam. The steam trains were expensive, so not many children owned them.

Lionel Trains

In 1900, Joshua Lionel Cowen formed a company to make toy trains in New York City. The company, called Lionel, still operates today. RailSounds II, which reproduces the actual sounds trains make, is one of its most recent developments.

Frank Hornby's Trains

In Britain and France, Frank Hornby's company, Meccano, Ltd., led the way in developing electric model trains in the 1920s. The electric models were sold alongside existing wind-up models. Over the next thirty years, electric train sets became the more popular. Today, people collect Meccano, Ltd., trains.

TIME LINE

1840s
The first toy trains are made of wood.

1870s
Tin trains can move by wind-up springs or steam.

1891
Marklin makes toy trains with tracks.

1900
Joshua Cowen forms the Lionel Manufacturing Company in New York.

1920s
Electric toy trains become more popular than wind-up models.

1935
Lionel introduces trains that make whistle sounds.

1994
Lionel's RailSounds II makes actual train sounds.

Skateboards

Skateboards are a fairly recent toy invention that quickly became one of the most popular. While many people skateboard for fun, skateboarding is also taken seriously as a sport around the world. Both adults and children enjoy skateboards.

Keep Covered!
Skateboarding safety is extremely important. Boarders should always wear helmets and, sometimes, knee and elbow pads, too.

From Skates to Skateboards

In 1760, Jean-Joseph Merlin, of Belgium, made the first pair of rollerskates. Nearly 150 years later, in the early 1900s, people began attaching rollerskate wheels to wood boards to make skateboards.

Surfing the Streets

Skateboarding became popular in the early 1960s when Larry Stevenson made skateboards that looked like surfboards. In 1963, Stevenson's company, Makaha, made the first professional skateboards in California. Within a few years, Makaha was making two thousand boards per day.

All about Wheels

Early skateboards had wheels made of clay. These wheels did not grip surfaces very well, and many skateboarders had serious accidents. Frank Nasworthy introduced plastic wheels in the 1970s, in Washington, D.C., and in California. These wheels made skateboards safer to ride.

TIME LINE

1760
Jean-Joseph Merlin makes the first rollerskates.

Early 1900s
People attach rollerskate wheels to wood boards to make "skateboards."

1963
The Makaha company, in California, makes the first professional skateboards.

1970s
Frank Nasworthy introduces plastic wheels that make skateboards safer.

1976
Florida builds the first skateboard park.

1993
ESPN introduces X Games. These games are the Olympics of extreme sports, including skateboarding.

Computer Games

Would you be surprised to know that computer games were not popular when they first appeared? Electronic games changed a lot in a short time to become the games of skill we have today.

Warning!
Always check the age rating on computer games and ask an adult for permission before you start playing a computer game.

Spacewar

The first computer game was called Spacewar. It was invented in 1962 by a team of scientists, led by Stephen "Slug" Russell, at the Massachusetts Institute of Technology.

In Your Hands!

In 1989, Nintendo invented a hand-held game **console** called Game Boy. Tetris, a puzzle game, was the most popular game to play on a Game Boy console. Today, Tetris is one of the best-selling video games of all time.

Through the Television

Since the 1980s, a lot of game consoles have been made, many of which use the television screen. TV game consoles include the Sony PlayStation, made in 1994, and the Microsoft Xbox, launched in 2001. In 2005, Sony developed the hand-held PlayStation. It is small enough to fit in a backpack or a briefcase, and it can be played silently, using headphones.

TIME LINE

1962
Spacewar is invented.

1974
The computer tennis game Pong becomes available for home use.

1980
Pac-Man is launched by Namco in Japan and released by Midway in the United States.

1989
Game Boy consoles and Tetris go on sale.

Early 1990s
CD-ROM games for home computers become popular.

1994
The Sony Corporation introduces PlayStation.

2001
Microsoft launches Xbox.

2005
Sony sells the portable PlayStation.

Other Inventions

People play with many kinds of toys and games. Some were invented such a long time ago that we do not know who created them. Building blocks, kites, and jump ropes fall into this group.

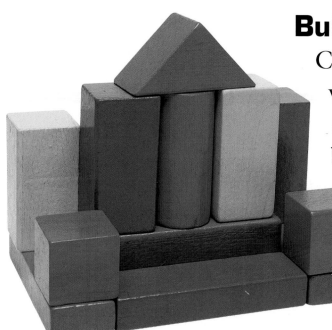

Building Blocks

Children have played with building blocks for centuries. At first, the blocks were stones, but later, in the **Victorian era**, blocks were made of wood. Today, children have a wide variety of building toys, from plastic Legos and K'NEX to magnetic Geomags.

Kites

Kites may have been invented by the Chinese as long as three thousand years ago. The first kites were made out of silk and bamboo. Today, there are many different kinds of kites, including stunt kites. Some of today's kites are made of nylon attached to **fiberglass** frames.

Jump Ropes

Jumping rope has been popular since the 1800s. Over the years, children have developed routines with rhymes and complicated footwork. The first jump ropes had wooden handles. Many jump ropes today are made of plastic.

PLASTIC

Plastic is one of the most common materials for making toys. Without it, many of the toys in this book would not be possible.

Plastic is used to make toys because it is tough, safe, waterproof, easily shaped, and can be made in many bright colors.

In 1951, two chemists in the United States, J. Paul Hogan and Robert L. Banks, "accidentally" discovered a type of plastic we still use today for making toys.

While these chemists were trying to make fuel, they noticed that their equipment had become clogged with a sticky, white substance. They recreated the white substance and realized that it was a new material — plastic!

Time Line

3500 B.C.
Ancient Egyptians play the board game Senet.

2000 B.C.
Egyptian children play with cloth dolls, marbles, and spinning tops.

600 B.C.
Ancient Egyptians play Alquerque.

A.D. 100
Ancient Greeks use yo-yos.

700
People play chess in India and Persia (Iran).

1100s
People use a wooden chess board to play checkers.

1200s
Children have wooden dolls.

1400s
Yo-yos are made of wood.

1700s
Jointed dolls are invented.

Dolls are made of wax.

1760
Jean-Joseph Merlin makes the first rollerskates.

1767
John Spilsbury makes the first jigsaw puzzle from a map.

1840s
The first toy trains are made of wood.

Dolls are made with soft fabric bodies and china arms, legs, and heads.

1870s
Trains are made out of tin and move by means of clockwork or steam.

1891
Marklin makes toy trains with tracks.

1898
Nikola Tesla demonstrates a radio-controlled toy boat.

1900
Joshua Cowen forms Lionel Manufacturing Company.

Early 1900s
The first skateboards are made.

The Dowst Brothers Company makes the first die-cast toy car.

Dolls are made of wood, china, fabric, and other materials.

1902
Morris Mitchom displays a "Teddy's bear" in his shop.

The Steiff toy company makes toy bears with jointed arms and legs.

1930
Donald Duncan buys a yo-yo company from Pedro Flores.

1931
Frank Hornby designs Dinky toys.

1933
In the United States, sales of jigsaw puzzles peak at ten million per week.

1940s
The first radio-controlled cars appear.

1950s
Lesney makes Matchbox cars.

Donald Duncan's toy company makes plastic yo-yos.

1951
J. Paul Hogan and Robert L. Banks discover a type of plastic.

1957
British Colonel H. J. Taplin flies the first radio-controlled airplane.

1959
Mattel produces the Barbie doll.

1962
The first computer game, Spacewar, is invented in the United States.

1970
Frank Nasworthy introduces plastic wheels to make skateboards safer.

1974
The computer game Pong is launched for home use.

1980
The video game Pac-Man is released.

1989
Game Boy consoles go on sale.

1993
ESPN develops X Games.

2005
Sony launches a handheld PlayStation.

Glossary

clay
a type of earth, soil, or mud that hardens when it is heated

competitions
contests or games played to win

concentration
focus; very close attention

console
the part of a computer game where the operating system is located

craze
a period of high popularity or of being in fashion; when a toy is in fashion, it is the latest craze

develop
to make or improve something gradually or over a period of time

device
a piece of equipment designed to do a certain task

die-cast
a type of metal that is shaped in a mold

fiberglass
a material made up of very fine glass fibers

geography
the layout and features of the land

Great Depression
the time from 1929 through the 1930s when the United States lost a lot of money, people were poor, and the effect spread worldwide

historians
people who study and write about history

inexpensive
does not cost a lot of money

jointed
made with joints, such as elbows, knees, hips, and shoulders

low-friction wheels
wheels that have little resistance between them and the surface they are moving on, which means the wheels can turn faster

mass-producing
making many copies of the same item, usually with the help of machines

opponent
the person or team someone plays against in a game or a competition

plastic
a long-lasting, waterproof
material used to make many
toys and other objects

propulsion
the act of propelling, or
moving an object forward

radio transmitter
an electronic device that sends
radio waves to a receiver

scale model
a miniature car, train, airplane, boat,
or other object made to look exactly
like the real, full-sized thing

three-dimensional
having length, width,
and height; not flat

Victorian era
the time between 1837 and 1901
when Queen Victoria ruled England

Further Information

Books

Toys and Games Then and Now. First Step Nonfiction (series).
  Robin Nelson (Lerner)

Toys! Amazing Stories Behind Some Great Inventions
  Don Wulffson (Henry Holt)

Web Sites

The Henry Ford Collections: Toys & Games.
  www.hfmgv.org/collections/collections/toys.asp

Museum of Childhood Kids' Pages
  www.vam.ac.uk/moc/kids/

Publisher's note to educators and parents: Our editors have carefully reviewed these
Web sites to ensure that they are suitable for children. Many Web sites change frequently,
however, and we cannot guarantee that a site's future contents will continue to meet our
high standards of quality and educational value. Be advised that children should be closely
supervised whenever they access the Internet.

Index